BABY LION

Published in Canada by Fitzhenry & Whiteside, 195 Allstate Parkway, Markham, Ontario L3R 4T8
Published in the United States by Fitzhenry & Whiteside, 121 Harvard Avenue, Suite 2, Allston, Massachusetts 02134

10 9 8 7 6 5 4 3 2 1

National Library of Canada Cataloguing in Publication
Lang, Aubrey
Baby lion / text by Aubrey Lang ; photography by Wayne Lynch.

(Nature babies)
ISBN 1-55041-711-8 (bound).--ISBN 1-55041-713-4 (pbk.)

1. Lions--Infancy--Juvenile literature. I. Lynch, Wayne II. Title. III. Series.

QL737.C23L34 2002   j599.757'139   C2002-901613-4

U.S. Cataloging-in-Publication Data
Library of Congress Standards

Lang, Aubrey.
Baby lion / text by Aubrey Lang ; photography by Wayne Lynch. -- 1st ed.
[32] p. : col. photos. ; cm.   (Nature babies)
Summary: Secure in the protection of the pride, a baby lion discovers a world that is both exciting and dangerous.
But it is through play that the little lion learns the most valuable lessons of survival in the wild.

ISBN 1-55041-711-8
ISBN 1-55041-713-4(pbk.)

1. Lions -- Juvenile literature. [1. Lions.] I. Lynch, Wayne, 1948- . II. Title. III. Series.
599.757 [E] 21   2002   CIP

Fitzhenry & Whiteside acknowledges with thanks the Canada Council for the Arts, the Government of Canada through the Book
Publishing Industry Development Program (BPIDP), and the Ontario Arts Council for their support for our publishing program.

Design by Wycliffe Smith
Printed in Hong Kong

BABY LION

Text by Aubrey Lang
Photography by Wayne Lynch

Fitzhenry & Whiteside

BEFORE YOU BEGIN

Dear Reader,

We love to watch and photograph wild animals--especially baby animals. We wrote this book to share with you some of the adventures in the life of a baby lion.

Whenever we were around a lion family, we were always careful not to harm or upset them in any way. To photograph the lions in this book, we spent many weeks living in East Africa. Lions move around at night, so each morning we had to search for them. Our car was small, and the windows were so low that a male lion standing next to the car could stick his head inside. Of course we kept the windows closed and photographed through a hatch in the roof!

This book is dedicated to Pauline—for who she is, and all that she has done with quiet determination.

— Aubrey Lang and Wayne Lynch

Table of Contents

When people think of Africa they think of lions. Unlike most wild cats, which live alone, lions live in large family groups called prides.

When this story begins, it is a difficult time for the lions of the Serengeti grasslands of East Africa. Many of the zebras, wildebeests and antelopes—which the lions usually hunt—have left the area. Food is scarce, and the lions and their cubs are often hungry.

In the Bila Shaka lion pride there are six adult females. It is unusual for the whole pride to be together at one time. The females, called lionesses, are the hunters of the pride. A lioness hunts alone for smaller animals. But two or three lionesses may work together when they hunt large, strong animals like zebras and African buffaloes.

Two adult males rule the pride. Male lions are larger and stronger than females. The thick, shaggy manes around their head make them look even bigger and more frightening. The males roar, patrol the family territory, and spray smelly urine on bushes and trees—a warning that all strangers should stay away. The big males will fight fiercely to protect the pride from outsiders.

A mother lion leaves the pride when she is ready to have her babies. She searches for some bushes or tall grass where she can be alone and hide her new cubs. Even before the cubs can open their eyes, they find their mother's milk. The cubs are always hungry and never want to stop nursing.

After a week, when their eyes open, the cubs begin to explore.

When the mother goes hunting, she usually leaves her cubs alone. But today an older brother baby-sits the youngsters. The cubs like to play, but the older sibling doesn't know his own strength. Sometimes he's a little rough. When he rolls on them or bites them too hard, the cubs meow and snarl.

15

Many of the females in the Bila Shaka pride have cubs. When the little ones are about a month old, the mothers and cubs join together. Often the adult females in a pride are sisters or cousins, and they nurse and care for each other's babies. A hungry cub might go from one mother to the next to fill its belly with warm milk.

The mother lions have not eaten in over two days. They must hunt for food. This time the cubs will have no baby sitter. The adult males, who often travel on their own, are nowhere in sight. Without adults to protect them, the young ones could be attacked by predators, like this hungry spotted hyena. Predators kill many lion cubs when the adult members of the pride are not around to defend them.

The mothers return shortly after sunrise. The hungry cubs rush out to greet them—a very important part of pride behavior. A cub rubs her cheek against her mother's face, then slowly rubs her whole body—including her tail—under the lioness's chin.

The hunt was not a success. The mothers walked a long way during the night and they are tired. All they want to do is sleep.

Three nights have passed, yet the mother lions still have not found a meal. Without food, the lionesses produce less milk, so the cubs don't have as much to eat either. The hungry cubs get cranky, and they fight when they are nursing. During the fight, one of the cubs accidentally digs his needle-sharp claws into his mother. She roars at him in anger.

photo credit: Buff & Gerald Corsi

One of the male rulers of the Bila Shaka pride has also returned with the lionesses. The young cubs look especially small beside the big male. But the male's size doesn't stop the cubs from chewing on his mane, pawing his face, and tugging on his tail like it was an old piece of rope.

This morning, the male lion is more patient with the cubs than their mothers.

At midday, the whole pride settles down for a snooze. Lions never waste energy, and they spend more time sleeping than doing anything else. Some of the mothers rest in the shade with their cubs. One lioness climbs a dead tree to escape from her nagging youngsters. Three of the older cubs also climb up the tree to enjoy the cool breeze.

Since their nighttime hunts have failed, the hungry pride goes hunting again in the late afternoon. They chase a large male warthog, but the speedy animal escapes down a burrow. Immediately, the lions start to dig after the warthog. They must be careful; warthogs have very sharp tusks that can slash and harm them. After an hour of frantic digging, the tired lionesses give up.

The family goes hungry again.

Stopping at a gully for a drink, the pride surprises an unlucky wildebeest. Soon there is food for everyone. The lionesses are the first to eat. They stuff themselves until they are full—only then are the cubs allowed some meat. When the pride has finished the meal, nothing but bones remain.

It is now a year later. The cubs of the Bila Shaka pride have grown into strong young lions. The female lions usually stay with the family pride for the rest of their life.

Young male lions are driven away. The outcasts travel alone or in small gangs until they are five or six years old. Then finally they may rule a pride of their own.

DID YOU KNOW?

- Male lions weigh an average of 425 pounds (193 kilograms). The females average 250 pounds (114 kilograms). The average male lion is 47 inches (119 centimeters) tall at the shoulder—about as high as a man's waist. Among the cats, only the tiger is larger.

- Both male and female lions roar. The sound carries up to five miles (eight kilometers).

- Lions roar to advertise their territory, locate pride members, strengthen friendships, and frighten outsiders.

- The mane on an adult male lion can be short and scraggly or long and bushy. The mane also can be blond, brown, rust or black. The mane is most developed when the male is in his prime at the age of five or six years.

- The lion's favorite prey is wildebeests or zebras.

- Today, lions live south of the Sahara Desert in eastern and southern Africa, and in a small area of northwestern India. In the past they roamed throughout Africa and the Middle East. During the last glaciation, lions even lived in North and South America, from Alaska to Peru. The Ice Age lion was a quarter larger than the present day lion.

- Stalking is a lion's favorite way to hunt. Usually they sneak up to within 100 feet (30 meters) of the prey before rushing at it. Lions are powerful cats, but they don't have the stamina to run more than 3-400 yards, (275-365 meters). They will usually give up rather than run any farther.

- Like most carnivores, lions will scavenge as well as hunt. They also frequently steal prey from leopards, cheetahs, and hyenas. They watch the movements of vultures and listen for the noisy feeding calls of hyenas to locate carcasses.

INDEX

A
Africa, 7, 34

B
baby-sitting, 14
behavior, 20

C
carnivores, 34
cubs, 12, 16, 18

F
feeding, 30
females, 8, 16, 32, 34
fighting, 10
food, 7, 30, 34

G
giving birth, 12

H
habitat, 34
hunger, 7, 12, 22, 28
hunting, 8, 28, 34

I
Ice Age, 34

L
lionesses, 8

M
male young, 32
males, 10, 18, 24, 34
manes, 10, 34
mother lions, 12, 16, 22

N
nursing, 12, 16

P
play, 14
predators, 18
prey, 8, 34
prides, 7, 8
prime, 34
protecting, 10

R
roaring, 34

S
scavenging, 34
Serengeti
    grasslands, 7
size, 34
sleeping, 26
stalking, 34
stamina, 34

T
tigers, 34

U
urine, 10

V
warthogs, 28
weight, 34

BIOGRAPHIES

When Dr. Wayne Lynch met Aubrey Lang, he was an emergency doctor and she was a pediatric nurse. Within five years they were married and had left their jobs in medicine to work together as writers and wildlife photographers. For more than twenty years they have explored the great wilderness areas of the world—tropical rainforests, remote islands in the Arctic and Antarctic, deserts, mountains, and African grasslands.

Dr. Lynch is a popular guest lecturer and an award-winning science writer. He is the author of more than two dozen titles for adults and children. His books cover a wide range of subjects, from the biology and behavior of penguins and northern bears, arctic and grassland ecology, to the lives of prairie birds and mountain wildlife. He is a Fellow of the internationally recognized Explorers Club, and an elected Fellow of the prestigious Arctic Institute of North America.

Ms. Lang is the author of a dozen nature books for children. She loves to share her wildlife experiences with young readers, and has more stories to tell in the Nature Baby Series.

The couple's impressive photo credits include thousands of images published in over two dozen countries.

CHAPTER ONE

WE DID IT!

REJOICE ALL YOU LIKE. TURMOIL WILL *NOT* BE HAPPY.

ORDERS WERE NO FIRING UNLESS *FIRED* UPON, DEADLOCK.

HERE YOU ARE *AGAIN*, DISOBEYING ORDERS.

WE GOT RESULTS. HE WON'T KNOW HOW.

BUT HE *WILL*. I'LL *TELL* HIM. EVERYONE ELSE MIGHT BE SCARED OF YOU, DEADLOCK, BUT *I'M* NOT.

SECOND-IN-COMMAND WON'T COUNT FOR ANYTHING THE MINUTE TURMOIL FINDS OUT. YOU'RE AS GOOD AS—

SHKOW

WARS AREN'T WON BY OVERLY CAUTIOUS COWARDS.

IT'S TIME FOR NEW LEADERSHIP.

WHO'S WITH ME?

5

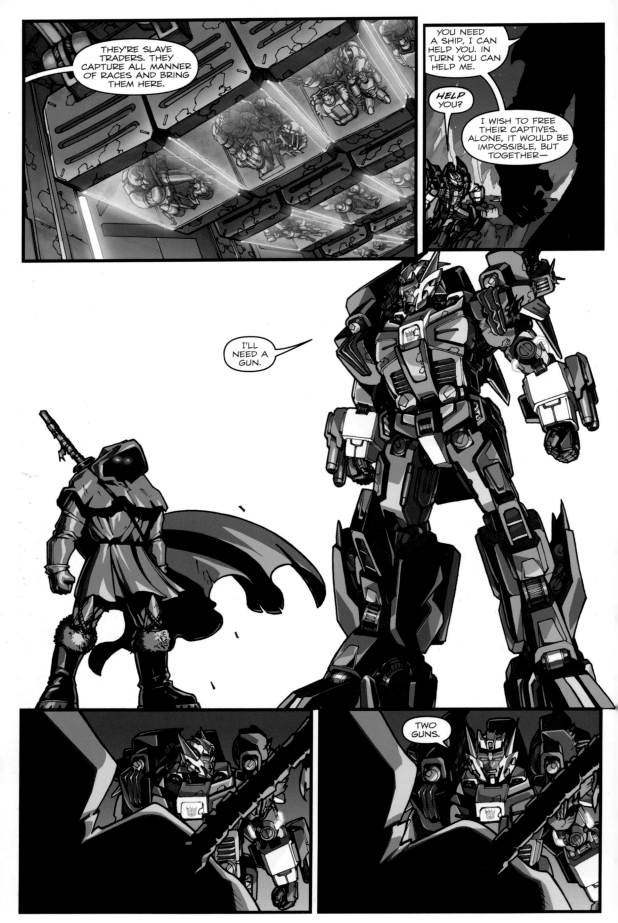

WE CAN STRIKE THE GUARDS ON THE UPPER PASS FIRST. YOU CAN USE THEIR ARMAMENTS.

ONCE WE FREE THE CAPTIVES, WE'LL COMMANDEER YOU A SHIP. YOU CAN TAKE THE CAPTIVES WITH YOU.

NOT LIKELY.

I CAN'T LEAVE THIS PLANET. YOU MUST DO THIS.

HELPING ANOTHER IS THE HIGHEST CALLING ONE CAN ASPIRE TO.

YOU SOUND LIKE AN AUTOBOT.

WHAT DOES AN AUTOBOT SOUND LIKE?

WEAK.

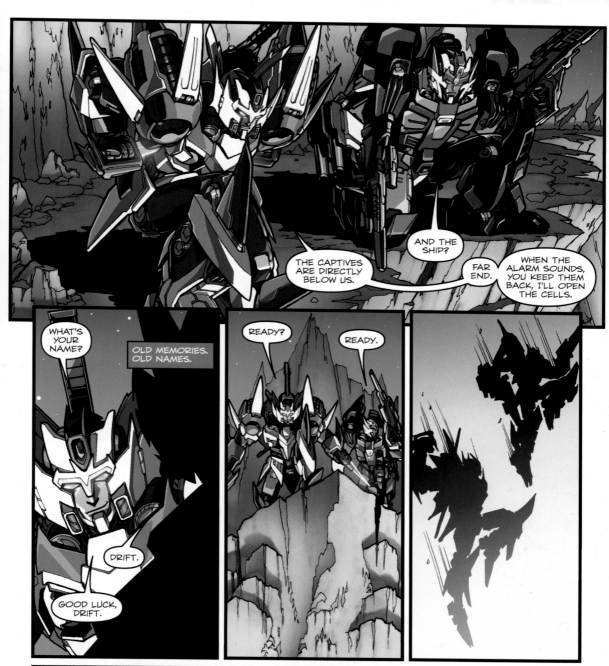

THE CAPTIVES ARE DIRECTLY BELOW US.

AND THE SHIP?

FAR END.

WHEN THE ALARM SOUNDS, YOU KEEP THEM BACK, I'LL OPEN THE CELLS.

WHAT'S YOUR NAME?

OLD MEMORIES. OLD NAMES.

DRIFT.

GOOD LUCK, DRIFT.

READY?

READY.

WOOP WOOP WOOP WOOP

ALARM! WE NEED TO HURRY!

REBUILT ME?! WHO *ARE* YOU?!

IT'S OKAY. YOU'RE SAFE. I TOOK YOU OUT OF THERE. YOU WOULD HAVE DIED.

TOOK ME OUT OF THERE? TO *WHERE?* WHERE IS THIS...

...PLACE?

I TOLD YOU, YOU'RE SAFE. NO ONE WILL HARM YOU HERE.

WELCOME...

"...TO THE NEW CRYSTAL CITY."

CHAPTER TWO

"IT WAS MORE HORRIFIC THAN WE COULD EVER HAVE ANTICIPATED.

"TWO FACTIONS AT WAR.

"AND SO MANY EAGER TO CHOOSE SIDES.

"BEFORE LONG, THE PLANET WAS ENGULFED AND THOSE REFUSING TO TAKE PART HAD LITTLE HOPE OF SURVIVAL.

"THE CIRCLE OF LIGHT WAS CONVENED.

"THE DECISION WAS MADE.

"AND UNDER THE COVER OF FIRE AND PAIN AND DEATH, WE SLIPPED AWAY."

"TO BEGIN WITH, WE DIDN'T GO FAR.

"BUT WHEN THE WAR SPREAD OUT TO OTHER PLANETS AND SYSTEMS, WE REALIZED WE'D HAVE TO TAKE MORE EXTREME MEASURES.

"WE FOUND SOMEWHERE NEW, SOMEWHERE INCONSPICUOUS AND HIDDEN...

"...UNDERGROUND."

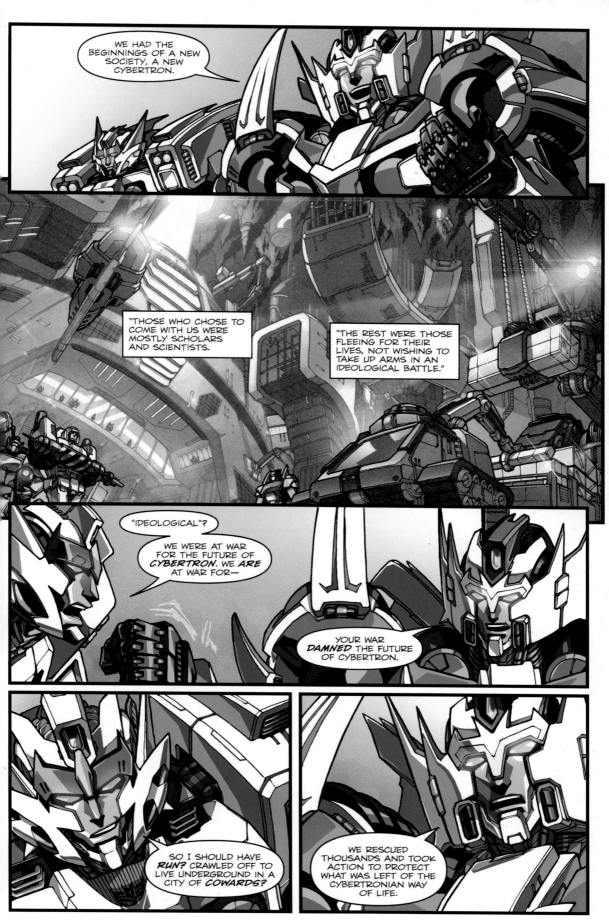

WE HAD THE BEGINNINGS OF A NEW SOCIETY, A NEW CYBERTRON.

"THOSE WHO CHOSE TO COME WITH US WERE MOSTLY SCHOLARS AND SCIENTISTS.

"THE REST WERE THOSE FLEEING FOR THEIR LIVES, NOT WISHING TO TAKE UP ARMS IN AN IDEOLOGICAL BATTLE."

"IDEOLOGICAL"?

WE WERE AT WAR FOR THE FUTURE OF *CYBERTRON*. WE *ARE* AT WAR FOR—

YOUR WAR *DAMNED* THE FUTURE OF CYBERTRON.

SO I SHOULD HAVE *RUN?* CRAWLED OFF TO LIVE UNDERGROUND IN A CITY OF *COWARDS?*

WE RESCUED THOUSANDS AND TOOK ACTION TO PROTECT WHAT WAS LEFT OF THE CYBERTRONIAN WAY OF LIFE.

LOOK AROUND YOU. THIS IS NO MERE *CITY*, THIS IS A *UTOPIA*.

"NO SICKNESS, NO POVERTY, NO ONE FORGOTTEN TO FALL BETWEEN THE CRACKS."

WHAT IS IT YOU'RE ACTUALLY FIGHTING FOR? WHAT IS IT THAT CONVINCED YOU TO TAKE UP ARMS?

YOU'RE NO RUN-OF-THE-MILL BRUTE. YOU BELIEVE IN SOMETHING, I CAN SEE IT.

YOU SEE NOTHING.

CYBERTRON WAS FALLING APART BEFORE THE WAR. OUR SOCIETY WAS SICK AND BLOATED AND ROTTEN.

DO YOU REMEMBER?

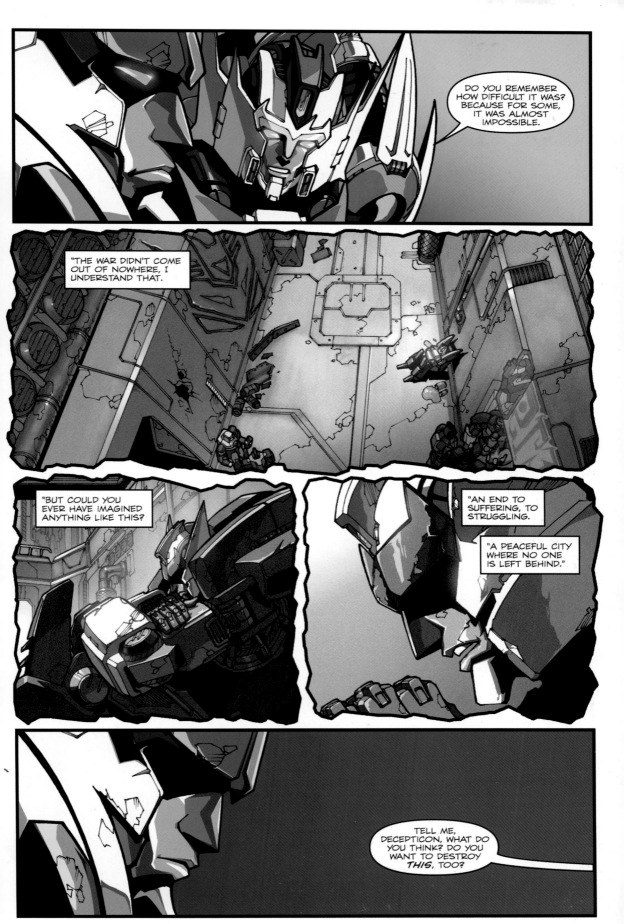

HIS WAYS COULD INFLUENCE OUR PEOPLE, WING.

HIS VERY PRESENCE COULD POTENTIALLY BRING MORE DECEPTICONS HERE AND WITH THEM THE WAR WE'VE FOUGHT SO LONG TO AVOID.

FOR NOW THE DECEPTICON IS *YOUR* RESPONSIBILITY. YOU WILL STAY WITH HIM AT ALL TIMES.

AND HE IS *NOT* TO BE EXPOSED TO THE PEOPLE OF THIS CITY.

VIOLENCE IS THEIR ONLY LANGUAGE.

IF HE BETRAYS US, IF HE DESTROYS WHAT WE HAVE HERE, THE BURDEN WILL BE YOURS AND YOURS *ALONE*.

HE WON'T BETRAY US. I KNOW HE WON'T.

AND HOW CAN YOU POSSIBLY *GUARANTEE* THAT?

31

TROUBLE IN PARADISE?

FOLLOW ME.

WHAT DOES THIS STAND FOR?

IT'S THE SYMBOL OF THE DECEPTICONS, YOU KNOW WHAT—

WHAT DOES IT *MEAN*?

STRENGTH, POWER, CONVICTION...

SUPERIORITY?

SO, YOU'RE THE BEST THEN—THE STRONGEST—AND BECAUSE OF THAT YOU SHOULD RULE?

YES.

PROVE IT.

NO GUNS, NO SWORDS.

PROVE IT.

WE'RE GOING TO DO THIS *EVERY* DAY. EVERY DAY, I'M GOING TO GIVE YOU A CHANCE TO PROVE ME WRONG.

IF YOU BEAT ME, YOU'RE FREE TO WALK OUT OF HERE.

IF YOU DON'T...

IF I DON'T?

YOU'RE HERE FOREVER.

AND YOU HAVEN'T?

SOME DEAL, YOU'VE HAD *YEARS* OF TRAINING.

NOT WITHOUT A GUN.

SO *LEARN*, DECEPTICON.

TOO SLOW.

WE'VE BEEN AT THIS FOR WEEKS, YOU'RE *STILL* TOO OBVIOUS WITH YOUR ATTACKS. *HIDE* YOUR INTENTIONS.

COME ON, DRIFT, WHERE'S ALL THAT DECEPTICON POWER AND SUPERIORITY?

IF YOU WANT TO CONQUER THE GALAXY, YOU NEED TO TRY HARDER THAN *THAT*.

THAT'S NOT WHY I JOINED.

WHAT?

THAT'S *NOT* WHY I *JOINED!*

I DIDN'T JOIN TO *"CONQUER"* ANYTHING.

I WAS *ALONE*, *DISCARDED* ON THE STREET WHEN I WAS FOUND, WHEN HE TOOK ME IN.

MEGATRON?

NO...

"...GASKET.

"HE WAS A LOT LIKE YOU, ANNOYINGLY OPTIMISTIC.

"HE BANDED US TOGETHER, GAVE US HOPE AND KEPT US ALIVE.

"WE WERE THE CITY'S REFUSE, NO ONE CARED IF WE LIVED OR DIED.

"THEY ONLY CARED WHEN WE STOLE THEIR PRECIOUS ENERGON.

"WE WERE STEALING TO LIVE, BUT THAT DIDN'T MATTER. IT *NEVER* MATTERED TO *THEM.*"

CALM DOWN, DRIFT. WE STEAL. WE BREAK THE LAW. AS FAR AS THE SYSTEM IS CONCERNED, *WE'RE* THE BAD GUYS.

IF IT WEREN'T FOR THEIR CORRUPT SYSTEM, WE WOULDN'T *HAVE* TO LOOK OUT FOR OURSELVES.

WELL, ONE DAY WE MIGHT —WHOA!

"I WAS FORCED INTO HIDING.

"BUT IT WASN'T LONG BEFORE NEWS OF MY ACTIONS REACHED CYBERTRON'S UNDERWORLD.

"I WAS TRAINED, PUT TO GOOD USE.

"AND LEARNED JUST HOW CORRUPT OUR SOCIETY'S ELITE *REALLY* WERE."

YOU SAID IT YOURSELF—CYBERTRON WAS ROTTEN TO THE CORE.

HOW MANY OF US WERE FORGOTTEN? HOW MANY WERE BEING LEFT TO DIE IN THE STREETS WHILE THE POLITICIANS GREW RICH?

SOMETHING NEEDED TO BE DONE. SOMEONE HAD TO MAKE A STAND.

THERE WAS ANOTHER WAY.

NO, THERE WAS *NO* OTHER WAY.

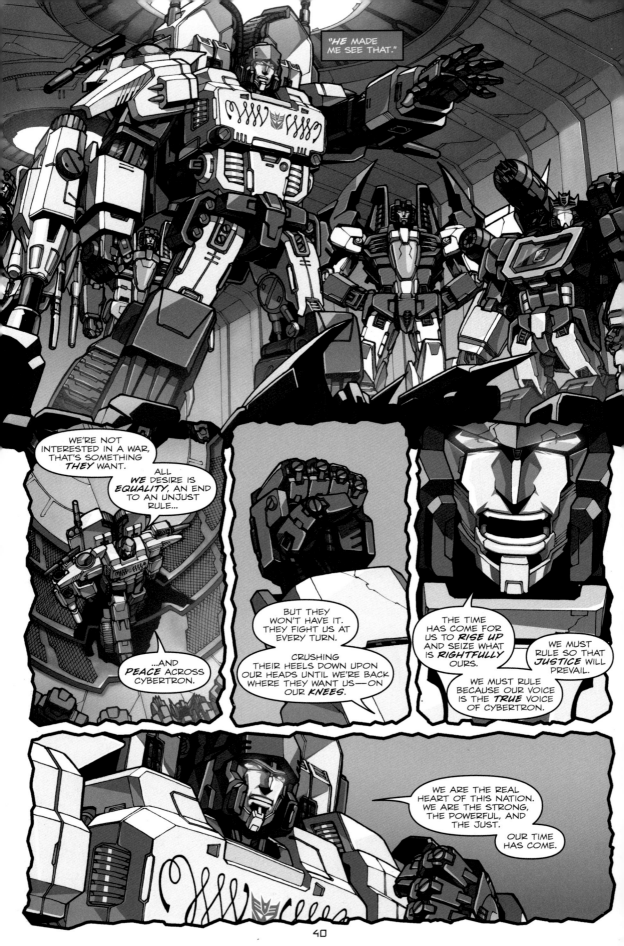

"*HE* MADE ME SEE THAT."

WE'RE NOT INTERESTED IN A WAR, THAT'S SOMETHING *THEY* WANT.

ALL *WE* DESIRE IS *EQUALITY,* AN END TO AN UNJUST RULE...

...AND *PEACE* ACROSS CYBERTRON.

BUT THEY WON'T HAVE IT. THEY FIGHT US AT EVERY TURN.

CRUSHING THEIR HEELS DOWN UPON OUR HEADS UNTIL WE'RE BACK WHERE THEY WANT US—ON OUR *KNEES.*

THE TIME HAS COME FOR US TO *RISE UP* AND SEIZE WHAT IS *RIGHTFULLY* OURS.

WE MUST RULE SO THAT *JUSTICE* WILL PREVAIL.

WE MUST RULE BECAUSE OUR VOICE IS THE *TRUE* VOICE OF CYBERTRON.

WE ARE THE REAL HEART OF THIS NATION. WE ARE THE STRONG, THE POWERFUL, AND THE JUST.

OUR TIME HAS COME.

43

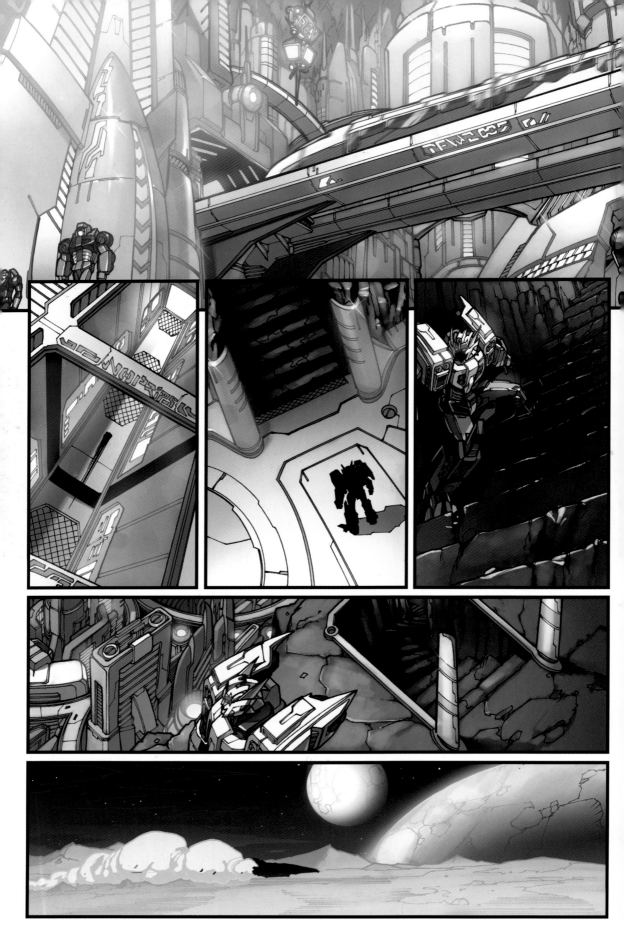

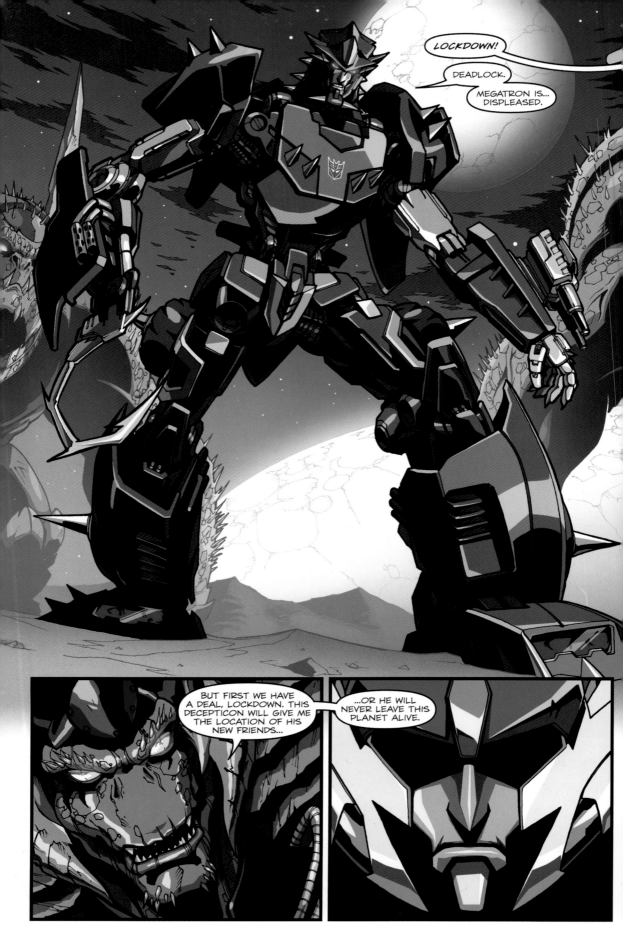

CHAPTER THREE

THERE COMES A TIME WITH ALL OF US. USUALLY WHEN IT'S QUIET, WHEN IT'S STILL.

A TIME WHERE WE ASK OURSELVES WHY.

WHY DO WE DO THIS? WHY DO WE FIGHT?

WHAT DID WE HOPE TO ACHIEVE? AND, PERHAPS MORE IMPORTANTLY...

...HOW FAR WILL WE GO TO GET WHAT WE WANT?

DRIFT!

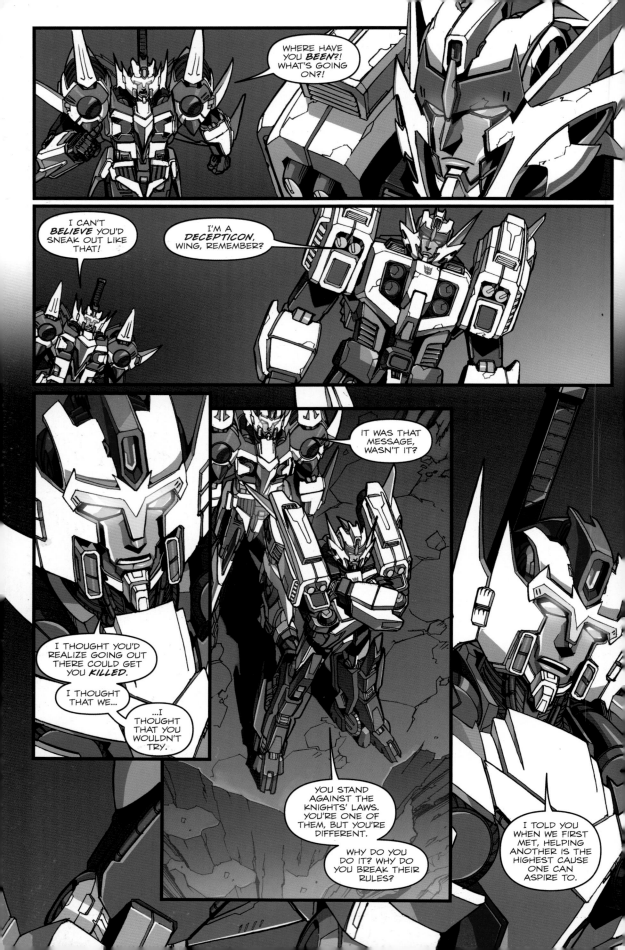

I DO IT BECAUSE I THINK IT'S RIGHT.

WHERE ARE YOU GOING?!

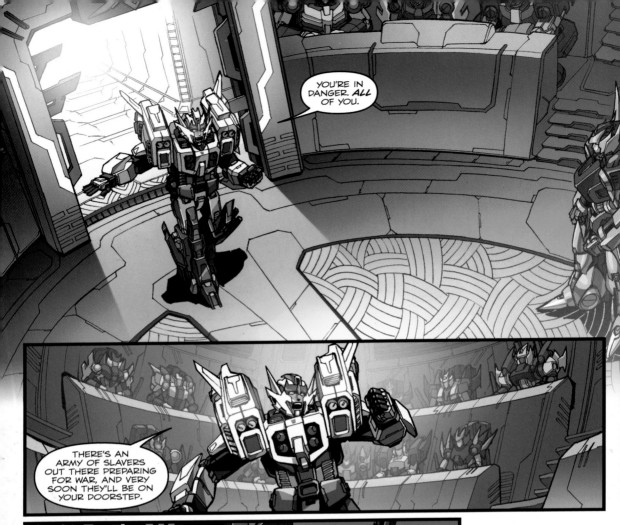

"I UNDERSTAND YOU ARE A GREAT DECEPTICON WARRIOR.

"FEARED.

"RESPECTED.

"CLEARLY YOU ARE A CUNNING WARRIOR..."

51

YOU *WOUND* ME.

MY KIND, LIKE YOURS, HAS EXISTED FOR SO *MANY* YEARS. WE *TOO* FELT THE STING OF ENDLESS WAR.

AS THE DUST SETTLED, WHAT WAS LEFT WAS A STRONGER, MORE *DETERMINED* SPECIES WITH ONE MISSION...

...IMMORTALITY.

"WE COMB THE GALAXIES IN SEARCH OF LIFEFORMS WE CAN USE. WE ADAPT OURSELVES AND GROW WITH EACH NEW DISCOVERY.

"YOU MIGHT CALL THEM UPGRADES."

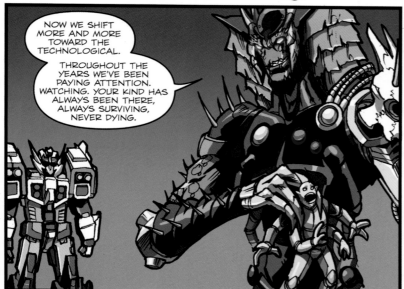

NOW WE SHIFT MORE AND MORE TOWARD THE TECHNOLOGICAL.

THROUGHOUT THE YEARS WE'VE BEEN PAYING ATTENTION. WATCHING. YOUR KIND HAS ALWAYS BEEN THERE, ALWAYS SURVIVING, NEVER DYING.

I WANT WHAT YOU HAVE.

53

I DON'T NEED *YOU*; YOUR HEROIC *"FRIENDS"* WILL DO. THEY'RE CLEARLY NOT DECEPTICONS, SO YOU SHOULDN'T MIND.

YOU'VE BEEN REPAIRED—THAT TAKES PARTS, EQUIPMENT. THERE'S MORE THAN THE ONE WHO SAVED YOU.

HOW MANY?

THEY'RE HIDDEN, *WELL* DEFENDED.

I HAVE AN ARMY.

AN ALL-OUT ATTACK WOULD BE SUICIDE.

THEN IT'S DECEIT.

GO TO THEM, TELL THEM WHATEVER YOU NEED, AND LEAD THEM INTO AN AMBUSH.

GIVE THEM TO ME AND YOU'LL HAVE YOUR FREEDOM. YOU CAN GO BACK TO YOUR MEGATRON.

WHAT SAY YOU?

AGREED.

YOU HAVE *ONE* SOLAR CYCLE.

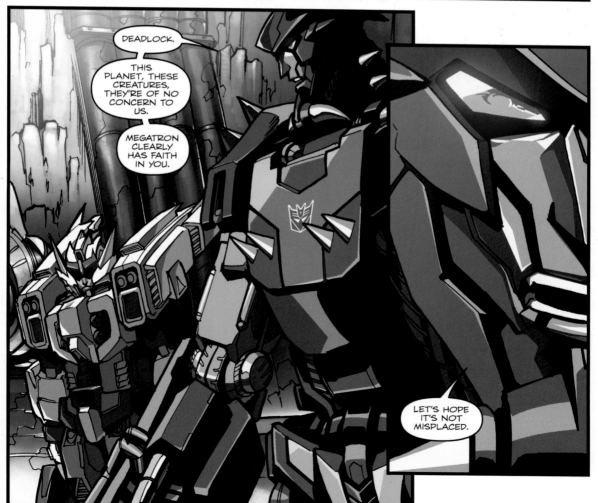

DEADLOCK.

THIS PLANET, THESE CREATURES, THEY'RE OF NO CONCERN TO US.

MEGATRON CLEARLY HAS FAITH IN YOU.

LET'S HOPE IT'S NOT MISPLACED.

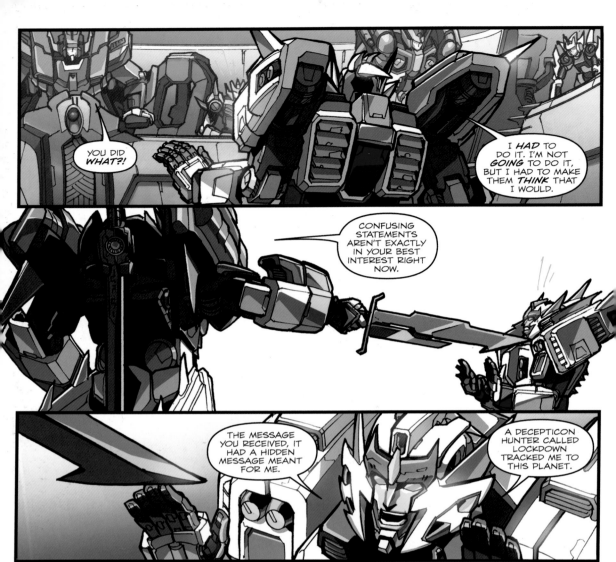

YOU DID *WHAT?!*

I *HAD* TO DO IT. I'M NOT *GOING* TO DO IT, BUT I HAD TO MAKE THEM *THINK* THAT I WOULD.

CONFUSING STATEMENTS AREN'T EXACTLY IN YOUR BEST INTEREST RIGHT NOW.

THE MESSAGE YOU RECEIVED, IT HAD A HIDDEN MESSAGE MEANT FOR ME.

A DECEPTICON HUNTER CALLED LOCKDOWN TRACKED ME TO THIS PLANET.

HE MADE A DEAL WITH THE SLAVERS, AND *THEY* MADE A DEAL WITH ME.

I *HAD* TO AGREE TO THE DEAL, THERE WAS NOTHING ELSE I COULD DO.

THEY'VE GIVEN ME ONE SOLAR CYCLE, WHATEVER THAT IS HERE, TO SEND THEM YOUR LOCATION AND LEAD YOU INTO AN AMBUSH.

AND WHAT WOULD YOU HAVE US DO?

PREPARE FOR BATTLE, DAI ATLAS. GO TO WAR. THEY DON'T KNOW HOW MANY WE HAVE HERE—

LOCK HIM UP!

THAT WON'T CHANGE ANYTHING.

I KNOW I'M A DECEPTICON. I KNOW YOU HATE ME, BUT I'M ON YOUR SIDE.

OF COURSE YOU ARE, RIGHT UP UNTIL YOU LEAD US INTO THAT AMBUSH.

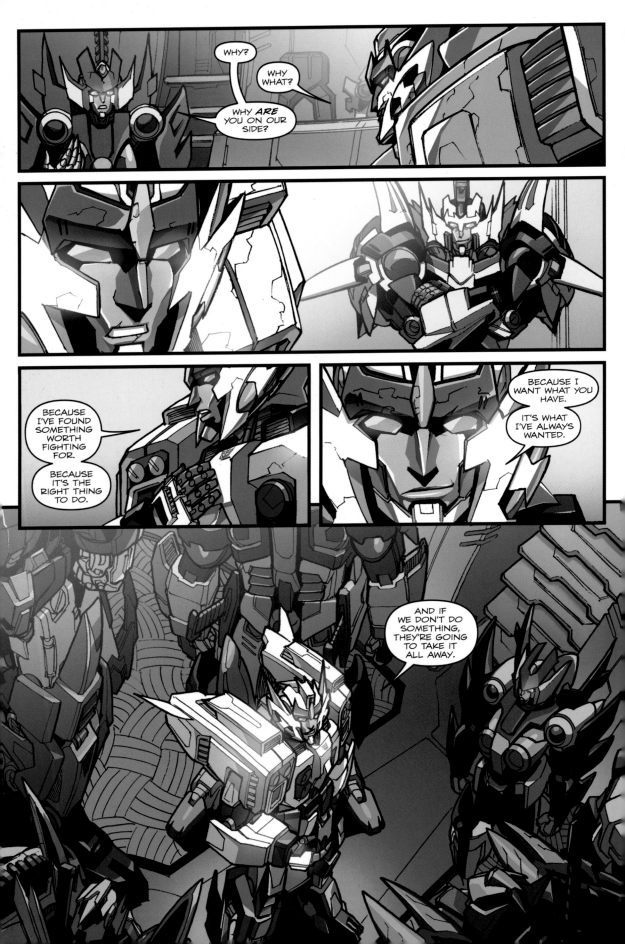

THEY KNOW YOU'RE HERE NOW. THE NUMBER-ONE REASON YOU'VE NEVER BEEN FOUND IS BECAUSE NO ONE HAS BEEN *LOOKING*.

BEFORE LONG THEY'LL FIND THIS PLACE. THEY'LL FIND IT, AND THEY'LL TEAR IT APART.

SURELY YOU HAVE WEAPONS...

WE DO. IN THE VAULT.

I *KNOW* THAT, I *KNOW*. BUT I'M *TRYING* TO FIX THIS. I'M *TRYING* TO MAKE IT RIGHT.

BY GOING TO WAR. *AGAIN*.

DOESN'T YOUR KIND THINK OF *ANYTHING* ELSE?

THIS IS *ALL* BECAUSE OF YOU! THIS IS *YOUR* FAULT!

I'M TRYING TO *SAVE* YOU.

LIKE YOU SAVED *CYBERTRON*?

...THEY KNOW *SOMETHING* IS OUT HERE, BUT THEY'RE NOT SURE WHAT.

THEY ONLY SAW ME.

DRIFT CAN SEND THEM A FALSE LOCATION. ONE THAT LEADS THEM TOWARD WHERE I'M HIDING, SOMEWHERE AWAY FROM THE CITY.

YOU'RE SUGGESTING GIVING YOUR OWN LIFE FOR CRYSTAL CITY?

YES.

IT WON'T WORK.

THEY KNOW YOU'RE NOT ALONE, THEY SAW I'D BEEN REBUILT.

I WAS CAREFUL NOT TO MENTION THE CITY, BUT THEY KNOW THERE'S MORE THAN ONE.

THEN LET THERE *BE* MORE THAN ONE.

WHAT ARE YOU DOING?

WHAT MUST BE DONE.

I WILL GO WITH WING. I WILL FIGHT.

YOU WILL DIE.

SO THE CITY MAY LIVE.

WE WILL GO.

MAYBE WE CAN CONSTRUCT A DERELICT SHIP TO MAKE IT APPEAR WE HAVE CRASHED HERE.

WE WON'T HAVE TO GO FAR. ONCE THEY FIND IT, THEY WON'T LOOK ANYWHERE ELSE.

THIS IS MADNESS. YOU WILL DIE, *ALL* OF YOU.

YOU SAID IT YOURSELF: WE ARE THE GUARDIANS OF CYBERTRON'S CULTURE.

IF THAT CANNOT BE SACRIFICED, THEN *WE* MUST.

WITH A FULLY ARMED CITY OF CYBERTRONIANS BEHIND US, WE COULD OVERCOME THE SLAVERS AND PUT AN END TO THEIR THREAT.

IT'S NOT AS THOUGH CYBERTRON HASN'T SEEN WAR BEFORE.

OUR CIVIL WAR WAS ONE THING. I CAN SEE WHY YOU MADE THE CHOICE YOU DID, BUT THIS IS DIFFERENT.

WHY ARE YOU DOING THIS?

IS THAT WHAT IT MEANS TO BE CYBERTRONIAN NOW? WAR?

IT'S ALL THE SAME.

I DON'T UNDERSTAND. WING TOLD ME YOUR HISTORY.

YOU'RE A SEASONED VETERAN, THE OLDEST OF THE KNIGHTS. YOU'VE FOUGHT IN WARS BEFORE, MANY WARS.

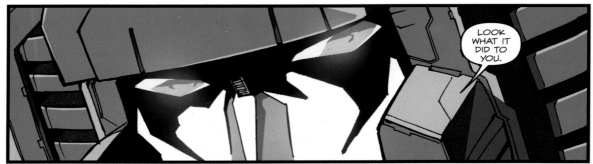

DRIFT.

WE NEED YOU TO SEND THE FALSE COORDINATES.

WE'VE FOUND SOMETHING WE CAN USE AS THE CRASHED SHIP.

IT WON'T TAKE LONG TO GET IT INTO POSITION, THEN WE'LL BE READY TO GO.

YOU KNOW, YOU DON'T NEED TO FIGHT WITH US. YOU COULD STAY HERE. ONCE THIS IS OVER, YOU'LL BE SAFE.

NO, THIS IS ALL MY FAULT. I NEED TO DO THIS.

WELL THEN, ONCE YOU SEND THOSE COORDINATES, YOU NEED TO COME WITH ME.

IF YOU'RE WITH US, YOU BETTER LOOK THE PART...

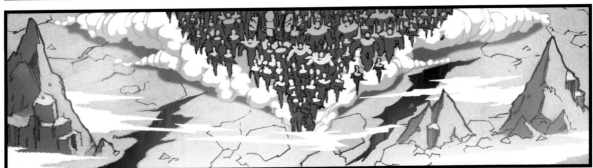

OH, HO! A NEW LOOK!

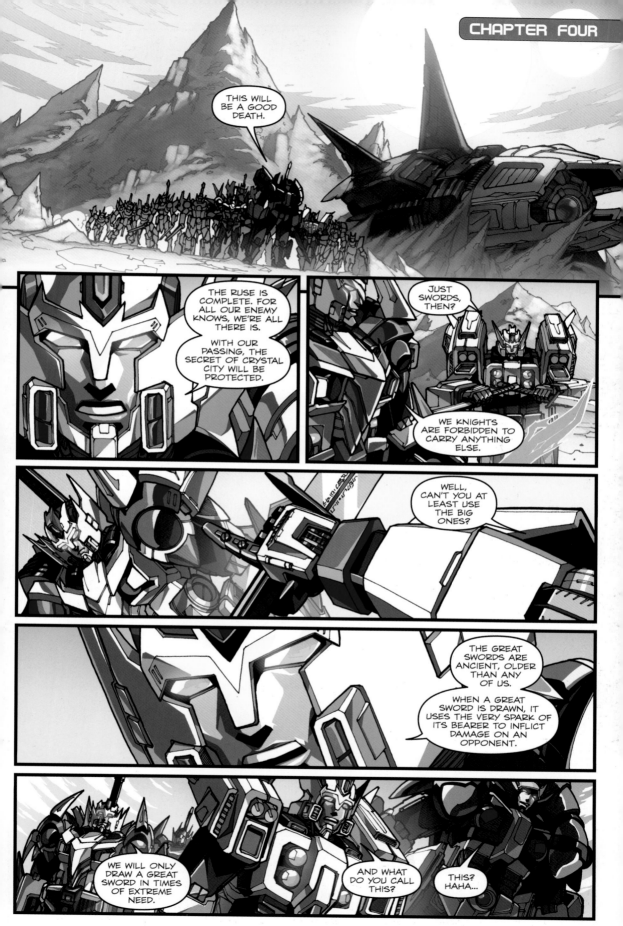

CHAPTER FOUR

THEY'LL HAVE NONE OF YOU, DRIFT. IF YOU PLAN ON BETRAYING US, NOW'S THE TIME.

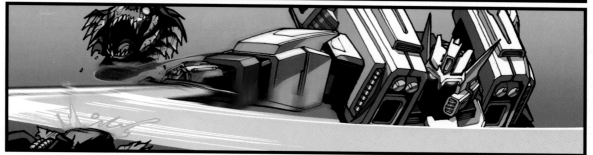

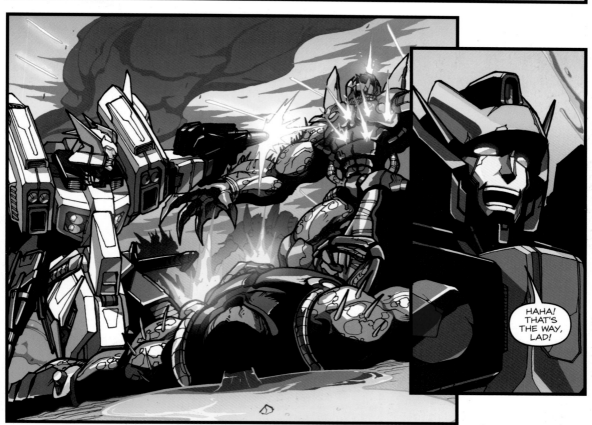

HAHA! THAT'S THE WAY, LAD!

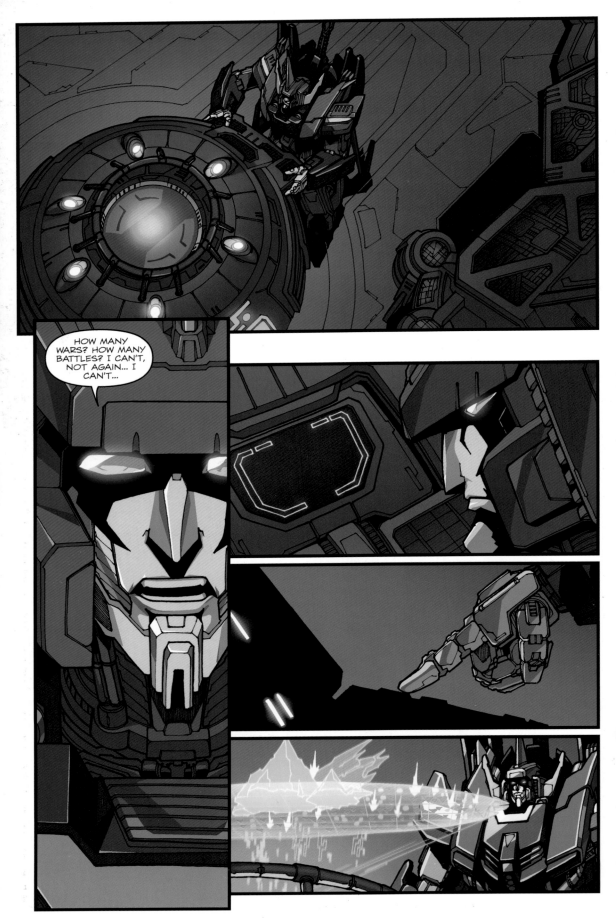

YOU.

HE'S THE LEAST OF YOUR CONCERNS.

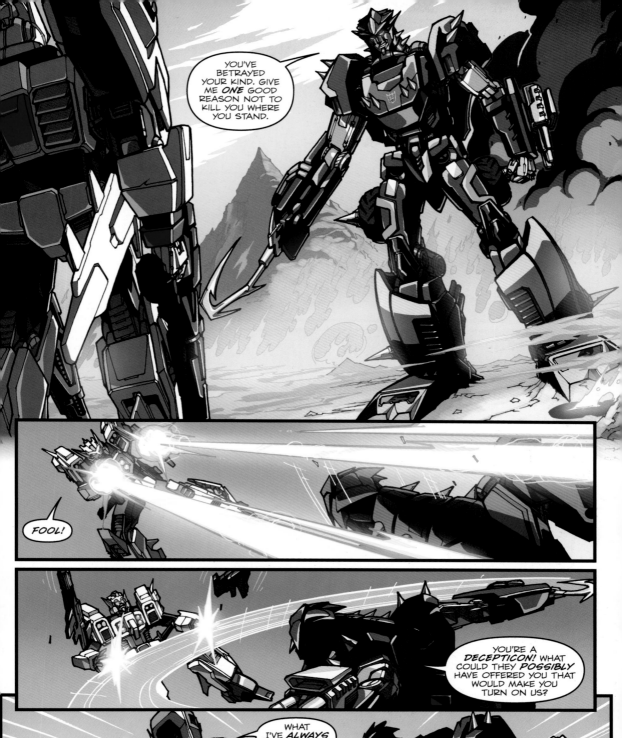

YOU'VE BETRAYED YOUR KIND. GIVE ME *ONE* GOOD REASON NOT TO KILL YOU WHERE YOU STAND.

FOOL!

YOU'RE A *DECEPTICON!* WHAT COULD THEY *POSSIBLY* HAVE OFFERED YOU THAT WOULD MAKE YOU TURN ON US?

WHAT I'VE *ALWAYS* WANTED...

...THE PROMISE OF A BETTER CYBERTRON.

NO!

HOW MANY?! HOW MANY MORE DO I NEED TO LOSE?!

AAARGH!

YOU'RE WOUNDED. SLOW.

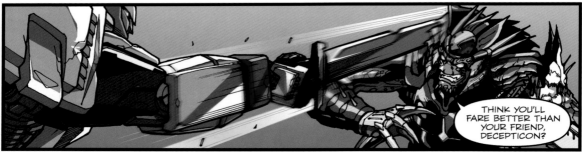

THINK YOU'LL FARE BETTER THAN YOUR FRIEND, DECEPTICON?

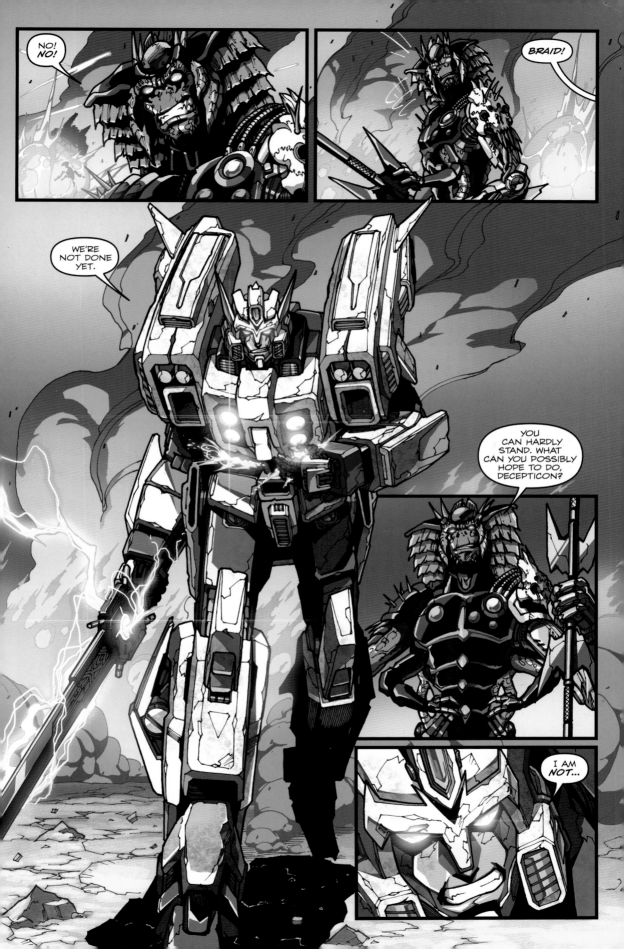

THIS COULD HAVE BEEN PREVENTED.

I WAS A FOOL.

CRYSTAL CITY WILL NO LONGER BE HIDDEN. WE WILL GROW. OUR MESSAGE OF PEACE WILL BE HEARD.

WILL YOU JOIN US, DRIFT?

I'M HONORED, DAI ATLAS, BUT I MUST REFUSE.

WHEN WE FIRST MET, I PROMISED WING I'D HELP HIM FREE THE SLAVES AND RETURN THEM TO THEIR HOMES.

THAT'S A PROMISE I INTEND TO KEEP.

AND THEN WHAT?

I'M NOT SURE.

I DON'T KNOW WHERE I BELONG ANYMORE. NOT WITH THE DECEPTICONS, OBVIOUSLY.

LOGIC WOULD DICTATE I JOIN THE AUTOBOTS, BUT... I'M NOT CONVINCED.

THEN TAKE THIS.

ALLOW IT TO SERVE AS A REMINDER OF WHO YOU ARE AND WHAT YOU HAVE ACHIEVED HERE.

NO MATTER WHAT YOU EVENTUALLY CHOOSE, REMEMBER TO STAY TRUE TO YOUR NEW PATH AND TO UPHOLD YOUR HONOR.

YOU WILL ALWAYS BE ONE OF US. THE WAR IS FAR FROM OVER, BUT EACH DAY WE TAKE ONE STEP CLOSER TO REAL PEACE.

AND WITH ANY LUCK, YOUNG KNIGHT, ONE DAY, FAR FROM HERE, YOU TOO WILL BE AT PEACE.

JAPAN. NOW.

THE END.

ART
GALLERY

Art by Alex Milne
Colors by Josh Perez

Art by Guido Guidi
Colors by Josh Perez

Art by Guido Guidi
Colors by Josh Perez

Art by Guido Guidi
Colors by Josh Perez

Art by Alex Milne
Colors by Josh Perez

Art by Guido Guidi
Colors by Josh Perez

Art by Alex Milne
Colors by Josh Perez

DRIFT

DRIFT – HEAD TWEAK 03

DRIFT

Sketches by
Alex Milne

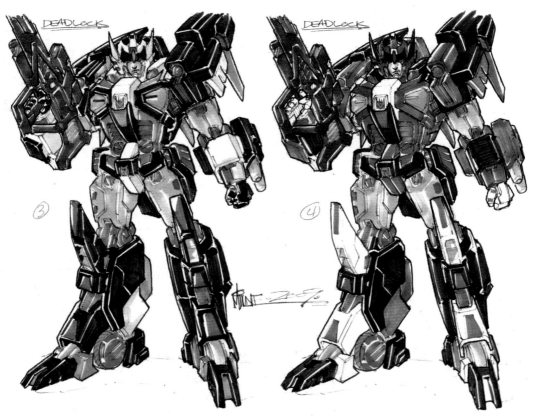

DEADLOCK

DEADLOCK

③

④

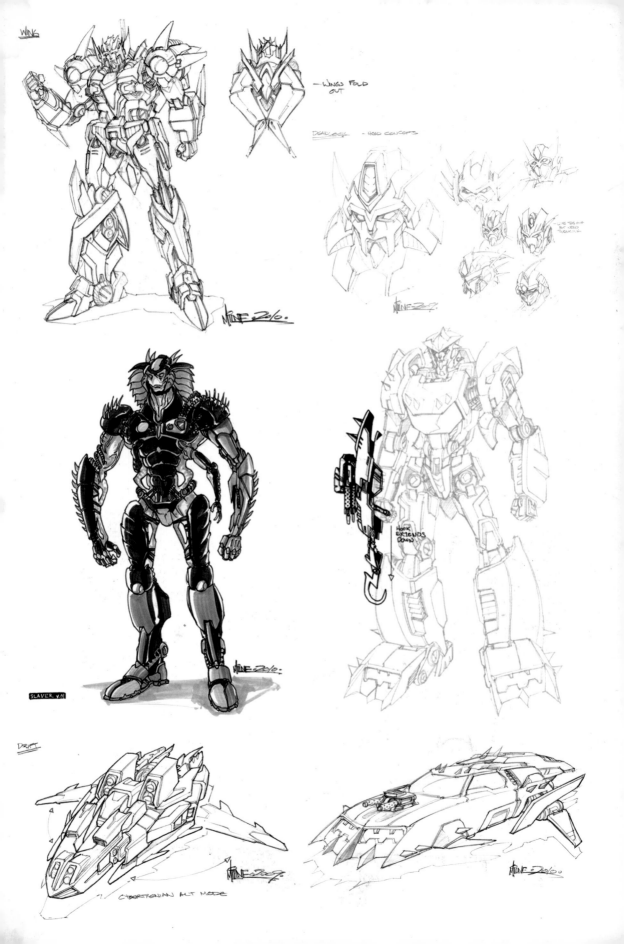

WING

— WINGS FOLD
OUT

DEADLOCK — HEAD CONCEPTS

HOOK
EXTENDS
DOWN

SLAVER V.M

DRIFT

CYBERTRONIAN ALT MODE

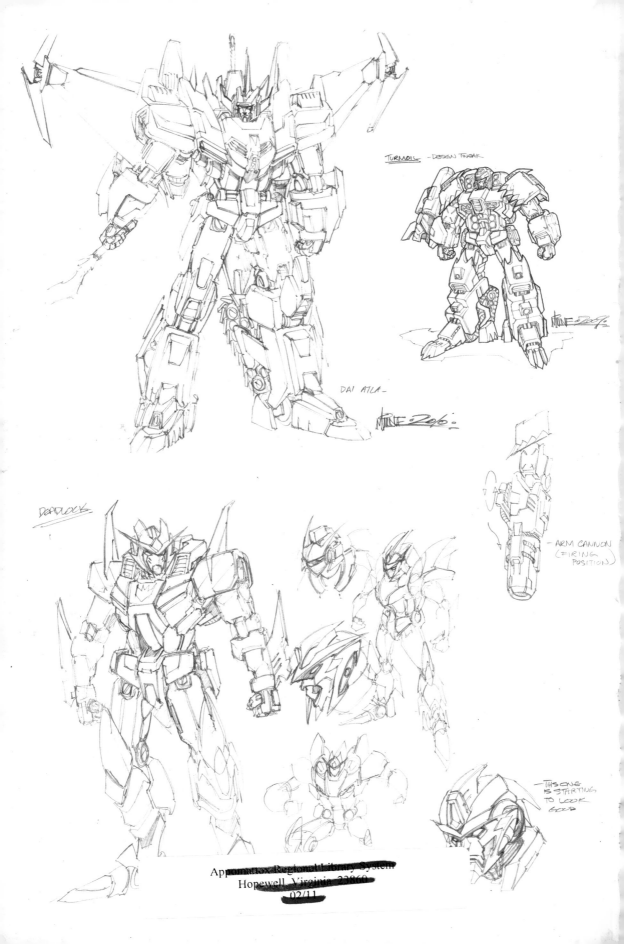

TURMOIL - DESIGN TWEAK

DAI ATLA -

DEADLOCK

- ARM CANNON
(FIRING
POSITION)

THIS ONE
IS STARTING
TO LOOK
GOOD